Mental Health Awareness

A Comprehensive Guide to Mental Health for Men

Dr. Jilesh

Copyright © 2023 by Jilesh Thilakan

Disclaimer: The information provided in this book is for general informational purposes only. The content is based on the topic of mental health awareness for men, but it should not be considered a substitute for professional medical, psychological, or therapeutic advice.

The reader understands and acknowledges that mental health is a complex and individualized field. This book is not a diagnostic manual, and it is essential to consult with qualified healthcare professionals or mental health experts for personalized evaluation, diagnosis, and treatment of mental health conditions.

The author and publisher disclaim any liability for any loss or damage incurred by the reader or any third party directly or indirectly as a result of the use or application of the information presented in this book. It is the responsibility of the reader to exercise personal

---

1. http://www.psychologyquill.com/

discernment and seek appropriate professional guidance when dealing with mental health concerns.

The book aims to raise awareness about mental health issues that men may face. However, mental health is a multifaceted and evolving field, and individuals may have unique experiences and needs.

About the Author

Dr. Jilesh is a renowned and highly rated Instructor on UDEMY, , psychotherapist manifestation expert, spell caster, life coach, and master of business administration. With extensive experience and expertise in the field, Dr. Jilesh has garnered a reputation as a trusted authority in the realm of manifestation and personal transformation.

As a highly rated manifestation expert and spell caster on Fiverr, Check Global Reviews here - https://www.fiverr.com/jileshthilakan?up_rollout=true[1] Dr.Jilesh has assisted countless individuals in manifesting their desires and achieving their goals. Through his deep understanding of the principles of manifestation, Dr. Jilesh has helped clients tap into their innate power to create their dream reality.

In addition to his work on Fiverr, **Dr. Jilesh has also excelled as a highly rated instructor on Udemy, with more than 30k students** Check his personal development courses here - https://www.udemy.com/user/jilesh-thilakan/ [2]sharing his knowledge and empowering students worldwide to harness the power of manifestation. With a passion for teaching and a commitment to providing valuable insights, Dr. Jilesh has garnered a loyal following of students who have experienced transformation and success under his guidance.

Dr. Jilesh's expertise extends beyond manifestation, as he is also a qualified psychotherapist and life coach. His background in psychology and counselling allows him to provide holistic support to individuals seeking personal growth and transformation. Through his empathetic approach and profound insights, Dr. Jilesh helps clients overcome challenges, break through limiting beliefs, and create lasting positive change in their lives.

Furthermore, Dr. Jilesh holds a master's degree in business administration, which adds a unique perspective to his work. His understanding of business principles and strategies allows him to guide individuals in aligning their personal goals with professional success, creating a harmonious balance between their aspirations and career pursuits.

With a diverse skill set and a genuine passion for helping others, Dr. Jilesh is committed to empowering individuals to unlock their full potential and manifest a life of abundance, fulfilment, and joy. Through his teachings, guidance, and transformative techniques, he aims to inspire and support others on their journey towards manifesting their deepest desires and living their best lives. **For more about Author checkout his Blog-** www.psychologyquill.com[3]

---

1. https://www.fiverr.com/jileshthilakan?up_rollout=true

2. https://www.udemy.com/user/jilesh-thilakan/

3. http://www.psychologyquill.com/

Introduction

In the bustling cacophony of modern life, where success is often measured by achievements and accolades, it is easy to overlook the quieter struggles that lie beneath the surface - the silent battles waged within the confines of one's mind. Welcome to "Mental Health Awareness: A Comprehensive Guide to Mental Health for Men," a journey into the depths of the human psyche, specifically tailored to empower and enlighten the stalwart souls who walk the path of manhood.

Imagine a world where mental health is not just a buzzword but an earnest priority, where emotional well-being is nurtured with the same fervour as physical health. In this labyrinth of emotions, we unlock the secrets that too often remain hidden in the shadows of societal expectations. Join us as we unravel the complexities and unveil the brilliance of men's mental health.

In these pages, we embark on a transformative expedition - a quest to redefine masculinity and liberate it from the confines of rigid stereotypes. Prepare to meet heroes who embrace vulnerability, warriors who wield the strength of compassion, and champions who dismantle the walls that isolate them from their true selves.

Our guide is a beacon of knowledge, illuminating the nuances of mental health, from its subtle whispers to its resonating echoes. We debunk myths, shatter stigmas, and build bridges of understanding. The canvas we paint is one of hope, resilience, and the enduring spirit that lies within every man.

In these stories, you will encounter familiar faces and strangers alike. Their journeys will mirror your struggles, and their victories will kindle the fire of inspiration. They are beacons of courage, their voices echoing across the ages, urging us to embrace our emotions and to forge a path towards healing.

As we traverse the landscapes of anxiety, depression, and trauma, we also find oases of peace, joy, and connection. It is a tapestry of emotions that weaves the fabric of the human experience. The pursuit of mental wellness is a pilgrimage with no destination - only a continuous evolution towards self-discovery and growth.

Dear reader, this is a guide not just for men, but for anyone who yearns to comprehend the labyrinth of the human mind. Our mission is to ignite the flame of awareness, fostering a world where mental health is not a burden but a gift - an indomitable force that propels us towards a brighter tomorrow.

So, brace yourself for the adventure ahead. Each page holds a revelation, each chapter an awakening. Let the symphony of emotions resonate within you, as we embrace the power of vulnerability and walk together on the path of Mental Health Awareness.

Chapter 1
Understanding Mental Health

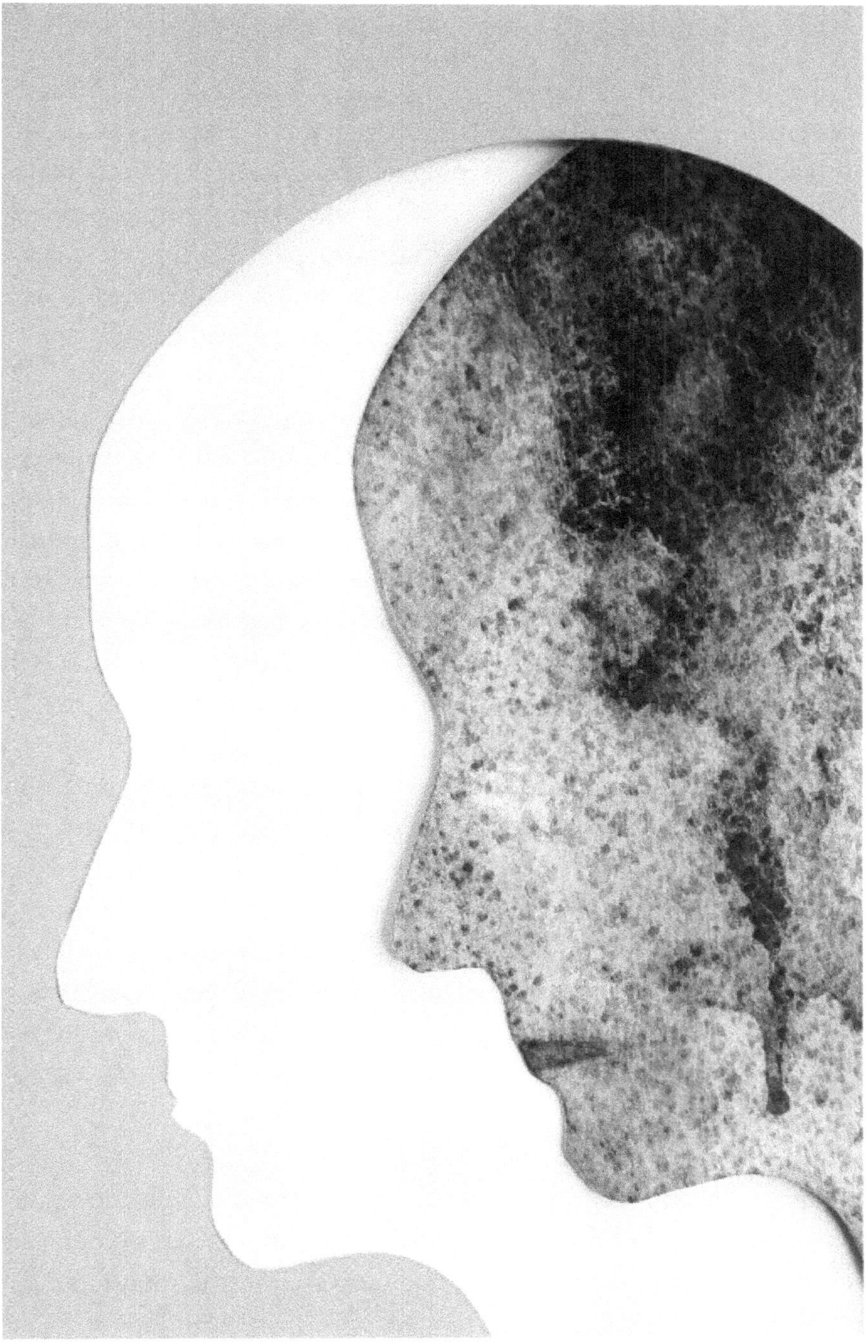

In the vast tapestry of human existence, the mind stands as an intricate masterpiece, weaving thoughts, emotions, and perceptions into the fabric of our reality. Within this complex labyrinth lies the essence of our mental health - a delicate balance that influences every facet of our lives. Welcome to the realm of understanding mental health, where we embark on a profound exploration of the mind's intricacies and the significance of emotional well-being in shaping our human experience.

The Definition of Mental Health:

At its core, mental health refers to the state of psychological and emotional well-being that allows individuals to cope with the challenges of life, build and maintain meaningful relationships, and embrace a sense of purpose and fulfilment. It encompasses the vast spectrum of human emotions - from happiness and contentment to sadness and grief, from confidence and joy to anxiety and fear. Mental health is not merely the absence of mental illness; rather, it is a dynamic continuum, with each individual's position on the spectrum continuously evolving.

The Mind-Body Connection:

In understanding mental health, we must recognize the profound connection between the mind and the body. The intricate interplay between our thoughts, emotions, and physical well-being shapes our overall health. Stress, for example, can manifest both mentally and physically, leading to a host of ailments if left unaddressed. Similarly, the impact of mental health on physical health is undeniable. Depression, for instance, can weaken the immune system and increase the risk of various medical conditions. Acknowledging this connection is crucial for comprehensive well-being.

The Importance of Mental Health:

Mental health forms the bedrock of our existence, influencing our capacity to navigate life's challenges, form meaningful relationships, and achieve our full potential. When our mental health is robust, we are better equipped to cope with stress, adapt to change, and make sound decisions. Moreover, mental well-being contributes to the cultivation of empathy, compassion, and resilience, fostering a healthier society that thrives on understanding and mutual support.

The Prevalence of Mental Health Issues:

Despite the universality of mental health, it is not immune to challenges. Mental health issues affect individuals of all ages, genders, and backgrounds. Statistics reveal the staggering prevalence of mental health disorders worldwide, with millions of people experiencing conditions such as depression, anxiety, bipolar disorder, and post-traumatic stress disorder (PTSD). Acknowledging the widespread nature of these challenges is crucial in promoting empathy, reducing stigma, and fostering a compassionate approach to mental health.

The Spectrum of Mental Health:

Understanding mental health requires acknowledging the diverse spectrum of human emotions and experiences. The spectrum spans from robust mental well-being, where individuals experience a sense of fulfilment, joy, and emotional resilience, to the other end, marked by mental illness, where individuals grapple with distress, dysfunction, and significant impairment in daily functioning. Between these extremes lie various states of mental health, each influenced by factors such as genetics, environment, and life experiences.

Resilience and Coping Mechanisms:

Resilience, the ability to bounce back from adversity, plays a pivotal role in mental health. Some individuals naturally possess higher resilience levels, allowing them to navigate through life's challenges with greater ease. Others may develop resilience through positive coping mechanisms, such as seeking support from loved ones, engaging in creative outlets, or practising mindfulness and meditation. Understanding and cultivating resilience can enhance our ability to withstand the storms that life may throw our way.

Factors Influencing Mental Health:

A myriad of factors shape an individual's mental health, contributing to the unique tapestry of their emotional well-being. These factors can be broadly categorized as biological, psychological, and social influences.

Biological Factors:

Genetics, brain chemistry, and hormonal imbalances play a significant role in mental health. Certain mental health conditions, such as schizophrenia and

bipolar disorder, have strong genetic components. Additionally, imbalances in neurotransmitters, the brain's chemical messengers, can impact mood, cognition, and behaviour.

Psychological Factors:

Individual experiences, perceptions, and thought patterns contribute to psychological well-being. Early childhood experiences, trauma, and attachment styles can influence how individuals perceive and respond to the world. Cognitive processes, such as irrational thinking or negative self-talk, can also affect mental health.

Social Factors:

The communities we belong to, our support systems, and the cultural norms surrounding mental health influence our emotional well-being. Social support is a powerful protective factor that buffers against the effects of stress and promotes resilience. Conversely, stigma and discrimination surrounding mental health can exacerbate existing challenges and deter individuals from seeking help.

The Impact of Childhood and Adolescence:

The early stages of life are pivotal in shaping an individual's mental health. Childhood experiences significantly influence the development of emotional regulation, social skills, and coping mechanisms. Adverse childhood experiences (ACEs), such as abuse or neglect, can have long-lasting effects on mental health and may increase the risk of mental health disorders later in life.

Similarly, adolescence, a period marked by rapid physical, emotional, and cognitive changes, is a crucial time for mental health. Teenagers often grapple with identity formation, peer pressure, and academic stress, all of which can impact their emotional well-being. Educating parents, caregivers, and educators about the unique mental health challenges faced by young individuals is vital in promoting healthy development and early intervention when needed.

The Role of Trauma:

Trauma, whether stemming from childhood experiences, natural disasters, or violence, has a profound impact on mental health. Traumatic events can trigger conditions such as post-traumatic stress disorder (PTSD), characterized by

intrusive memories, avoidance behaviours, and emotional numbing. Understanding trauma-informed care and its role in supporting individuals who have experienced trauma is essential in fostering healing and resilience.

Understanding mental health is a journey of exploration, empathy, and self-discovery. By acknowledging the diverse spectrum of emotions, factors influencing mental well-being, and the impact of childhood experiences and trauma, we lay the foundation for a compassionate and informed approach to mental health. Embracing this understanding, we foster a world where mental health is prioritized, stigma is eradicated, and individuals are empowered to embark on a path of healing and growth.

Chapter 2
The Impact of Gender Norms on Men's Mental Health

Since time immemorial, societies around the world have constructed intricate webs of expectations and norms surrounding gender roles. These deeply ingrained societal constructs define how individuals should behave, express emotions, and navigate the world based on their gender. For men, the pressure to conform to traditional masculinity norms can have profound implications on their mental health. In this chapter, we explore the impact of gender norms on men's emotional well-being, shedding light on the complexities of masculinity and its connection to mental health.

The Conundrum of Masculinity:

The traditional notion of masculinity often portrays men as stoic, strong, and emotionally restrained. From an early age, boys are taught to suppress emotions like sadness and vulnerability, and instead, embody traits of dominance, aggression, and emotional detachment. This conundrum forces men to adhere to a rigid mold, often denying them the opportunity to explore and express the full spectrum of their emotions.

Emotional Repression:

One of the most significant impacts of traditional masculinity on men's mental health is emotional repression. Society teaches boys that showing vulnerability or seeking emotional support is a sign of weakness. As a result, men may suppress their emotions, leading to a disconnect from their feelings and a sense of emotional isolation. Emotional repression can pave the way for unresolved trauma, increased stress, and the development of mental health disorders.

Expressive Limitations:

Traditional masculinity constrains men's emotional expression, leading to an inability to articulate their feelings fully. Men may struggle to communicate their emotional needs, leading to misunderstandings in relationships and an increased risk of social isolation. This inability to express emotions can lead to feelings of frustration, anger, and hopelessness, contributing to mental health challenges.

The Burden of Self-Reliance:

The stoic and self-reliant image of traditional masculinity may hinder men from seeking help during times of emotional distress. The societal expectation that

men should "tough it out" and solve their problems on their own can be detrimental to their mental health. Men may hesitate to seek professional support or open up to loved ones, fearing judgment or the perception of weakness.

Toxic Masculinity:

Toxic masculinity represents an extreme manifestation of traditional gender norms, emphasizing aggression, dominance, and the suppression of emotions. This harmful ideology perpetuates violence, misogyny, and homophobia, fostering an environment that is hostile to mental well-being. Breaking free from toxic masculinity is essential for fostering healthy relationships and cultivating a compassionate society.

The Connection between Masculinity and Risky Behaviours:

The societal pressure to conform to masculine ideals can lead some men to engage in risky behaviours as a means of validation or as a coping mechanism. Substance abuse, reckless behaviours, and avoiding seeking help for physical or mental health issues are examples of how this pressure may manifest. These risky behaviours can exacerbate mental health challenges and lead to a vicious cycle of negative outcomes.

Impact on Parenting and Fatherhood:

The impact of gender norms on men's mental health extends to their roles as fathers. Fathers may struggle with expectations of being the primary provider while also being emotionally available to their children. The pressure to be a "strong" and "unemotional" figure can hinder emotional connection and bonding with their children, potentially affecting the mental health of both the father and the child.

Challenging Gender Norms for Improved Mental Health:

The path to improved mental health for men involves challenging and redefining traditional masculinity norms. Encouraging emotional intelligence, vulnerability, and open communication can create an environment where men feel empowered to express their emotions and seek support when needed. Celebrating diverse expressions of masculinity can promote acceptance and understanding, fostering a healthier society for all genders.

Promoting Emotional Literacy:

Emotional literacy, the ability to identify and understand one's emotions, is crucial for men's mental health. By encouraging emotional intelligence from an early age and promoting emotional literacy in educational settings, we can equip men with the tools to navigate their emotions with confidence and self-awareness.

Breaking the Silence:

Creating spaces where men feel comfortable sharing their feelings and experiences is vital for combating the impact of traditional masculinity on mental health. Breaking the silence around mental health challenges can reduce stigma and empower men to seek help without fear of judgment or shame.

Promoting Positive Role Models:

Positive role models who challenge traditional masculinity norms and embrace emotional vulnerability can have a profound impact on men's mental health. By celebrating individuals who exhibit strength through emotional expression, we redefine masculinity and create new norms that prioritize emotional well-being.

The impact of gender norms on men's mental health is a multifaceted and deeply rooted issue. The pressure to conform to traditional masculinity can lead to emotional repression, expressive limitations, and the burden of self-reliance. Challenging these norms and fostering a culture of emotional intelligence, openness, and acceptance is vital in promoting men's mental well-being. As we work towards dismantling the harmful aspects of traditional masculinity, we pave the way for a future where men can embrace their full emotional selves, forging healthier connections and achieving greater emotional resilience. Through collective efforts, we strive to build a society that values mental health and supports every individual in their journey towards emotional fulfilment and self-discovery.

Chapter 3
Common Mental Health Challenges for Men

In the realm of mental health, the human experience is diverse, with each individual navigating their unique struggles and triumphs. For men, societal expectations, gender norms, and cultural pressures can influence the manifestation of mental health challenges. In this chapter, we delve into the common mental health issues that men may face, shedding light on the signs, symptoms, and potential risk factors associated with each condition. By understanding these challenges, we aim to empower men to recognize and seek support for their mental well-being.

Depression:

Depression is a prevalent mental health condition that affects people of all genders, but men may experience it differently due to the influence of traditional masculinity norms. Men with depression may be less likely to express feelings of sadness or hopelessness openly, leading to symptoms being overlooked or mistaken for other issues. Instead of expressing sadness, men may exhibit signs of irritability, anger, or reckless behaviour. Recognizing the diverse ways depression may manifest in men is crucial for early detection and intervention.

Symptoms of Depression in Men:

- Persistent feelings of sadness or emptiness
- Loss of interest in previously enjoyable activities
- Difficulty concentrating or making decisions
- Changes in appetite and weight
- Fatigue or loss of energy
- Thoughts of self-harm or suicide

Anxiety:

Anxiety is another common mental health challenge faced by men. While anxiety is a natural response to stress, excessive and uncontrollable worry can become overwhelming and interfere with daily life. Men with anxiety may feel pressured to "tough it out" and may be less likely to seek help for their symptoms. Anxiety can manifest differently in men, with some experiencing physical symptoms such as tension headaches or gastrointestinal issues.

Symptoms of Anxiety in Men:

- Excessive worrying or fear
- Restlessness or irritability
- Muscle tension or aches
- Difficulty sleeping or staying asleep
- Racing thoughts or difficulty concentrating
- Avoidance of certain situations or activities

Substance Abuse:

Substance abuse is often linked to mental health challenges, as individuals may turn to drugs or alcohol as a coping mechanism for emotional distress. Men, in particular, may face societal pressure to engage in risky behaviours, including substance use, as a means of conforming to traditional masculine ideals. Substance abuse can exacerbate underlying mental health conditions and lead to a cycle of dependency and negative consequences.

Signs of Substance Abuse in Men:

- Increased tolerance and need for higher amounts of the substance
- Withdrawal symptoms when not using the substance
- Neglecting responsibilities and hobbies in favour of substance use
- Legal or financial problems related to substance use
- Failed attempts to quit or cut down on substance use

Post-Traumatic Stress Disorder (PTSD):

Men may be exposed to traumatic events, such as combat, accidents, or violence, which can lead to post-traumatic stress disorder (PTSD). PTSD can significantly impact an individual's emotional well-being and daily functioning. The influence of traditional masculinity may deter men from seeking help for PTSD, leading to delayed diagnosis and treatment.

Symptoms of PTSD in Men:

- Intrusive memories or flashbacks of the traumatic event
- Avoidance of reminders of the trauma
- Emotional numbness or detachment
- Hyper-vigilance or exaggerated startle response
- Irritability or outbursts of anger
- Sleep disturbances

Suicide Risk:

Men face a higher risk of suicide, highlighting the urgency of addressing mental health challenges in this population. The pressure to conform to traditional masculinity norms may discourage men from seeking help, leading to untreated mental health issues. Suicide risk factors include a history of mental health conditions, substance abuse, previous suicide attempts, and access to lethal means.

Recognizing Suicide Warning Signs:

- Talking about wanting to die or feeling hopeless
- Increased substance use
- Withdrawing from friends and family
- Giving away possessions
- Drastic changes in mood or behaviour
- Expressing feelings of being a burden to others

Understanding the common mental health challenges faced by men is crucial in promoting early detection, intervention, and support. Depression, anxiety, substance abuse, PTSD, and suicide risk are among the issues that men may encounter, each influenced by the complex interplay of gender norms, societal expectations, and individual experiences. By challenging the stigma surrounding mental health and embracing a more compassionate approach, we can create an environment where men feel empowered to seek help without fear of judgment or perceived weakness. Together, we can foster a world where mental health is prioritized, and individuals are supported in their journey towards emotional well-being and resilience.

Chapter 4
Promoting Mental Wellness

In the realm of mental health, the journey toward well-being is not a passive endeavour; it is an active and empowering pursuit. Just as we care for our physical health through exercise and nutrition, we must actively nurture our mental well-being. In this chapter, we explore the concept of mental wellness and its significance in fostering emotional resilience and balance. From mindfulness practices and physical activity to creative outlets and social connections, we delve into practical strategies to promote mental wellness, empowering individuals to cultivate a positive and fulfilling inner landscape.

Mindfulness and Meditation:

At the heart of mental wellness lies the practice of mindfulness and meditation. Mindfulness involves paying deliberate attention to the present moment without judgment. Through mindfulness, individuals can become more attuned to their thoughts, emotions, and physical sensations, allowing them to navigate challenges with greater clarity and emotional intelligence. Meditation, on the other hand, encourages a state of deep relaxation and awareness, reducing stress and promoting emotional well-being.

Incorporating Mindfulness Into Daily Life:

- Engaging in mindful breathing exercises
- Practising mindful eating, savouring each bite
- Observing nature and connecting with the environment
- Engaging in mindful movement, such as yoga or tai chi
- Practising gratitude and appreciation for the present moment

Physical Activity:

The connection between physical and mental health is profound. Engaging in regular physical activity not only enhances physical well-being but also positively impacts mood and mental clarity. Exercise releases endorphins, the body's natural mood-boosters, which can reduce stress and promote feelings of happiness and relaxation.

Incorporating Physical Activity Into Daily Routine:

- Engaging in regular cardiovascular exercises, such as walking, jogging, or cycling

- Incorporating strength training exercises to build physical and mental resilience
- Participating in sports or recreational activities that bring joy
- Practising outdoor activities, such as hiking or gardening, to connect with nature

Creative Outlets:

Artistic expression can be a powerful tool for promoting mental wellness. Engaging in creative outlets allows individuals to channel emotions and thoughts in constructive ways, reducing stress and fostering self-expression. Whether through painting, writing, music, or dance, creative endeavours can provide a sense of fulfilment and catharsis.

Exploring Creative Outlets:

- Keeping a journal to process thoughts and emotions
- Trying out various art forms, such as drawing, sculpting, or photography
- Learning to play a musical instrument or engaging in singing
- Participating in group art or writing workshops for social connections

Social Connections:

Human beings are inherently social creatures, and fostering meaningful connections is vital for mental wellness. Building and maintaining strong social networks can provide emotional support, reduce feelings of loneliness, and increase overall life satisfaction. Social interactions also offer an opportunity for empathy and understanding, promoting a sense of belonging.

Nurturing Social Connections:

- Engaging in regular social activities with friends, family, or community groups
- Joining clubs or organizations based on shared interests
- Participating in volunteer work to contribute to the community
- Reaching out to others to offer support and build meaningful relationships

Balancing Work and Life:

The demands of modern life can often lead to a lack of balance between work and personal life, which can adversely impact mental wellness. Finding ways to

create a healthy work-life balance is essential for reducing stress and preventing burnout.

Strategies for Achieving Work-Life Balance:

- Setting boundaries between work and personal time
- Prioritizing self-care and taking breaks during the workday
- Engaging in hobbies and activities outside of work to recharge
- Communicating openly with employers or supervisors about workload and expectations

Seeking Professional Support:

Promoting mental wellness also involves recognizing when professional support is needed. Just as we seek medical attention for physical health concerns, seeking therapy or counselling for mental health challenges is a proactive step toward emotional well-being. Mental health professionals can provide tools and guidance to navigate through difficult emotions and life transitions.

When to Seek Professional Support:

- When experiencing persistent feelings of sadness or anxiety
- When facing significant life changes or trauma
- When coping mechanisms become maladaptive or harmful
- When daily functioning is impaired by mental health challenges

Promoting mental wellness is an ongoing journey of self-discovery, self-compassion, and growth. The integration of mindfulness and meditation, physical activity, creative outlets, social connections, and work-life balance lays the foundation for a resilient and balanced emotional landscape. By nurturing mental wellness, individuals equip themselves with the tools to navigate life's challenges with grace and emotional intelligence.

In the pursuit of mental well-being, we must also recognize the value of seeking professional support when needed. Therapists, counsellors, and mental health professionals serve as compassionate guides, empowering individuals to overcome mental health challenges and embrace their true selves.

As we traverse the path of mental wellness, let us remember that it is a journey

of self-acceptance, vulnerability, and growth. Embracing our emotions and nurturing our inner world allows us to flourish, creating a ripple effect of positivity in our relationships, communities, and the world at large. Together, let us cultivate mental wellness, fostering a society where emotional well-being is valued and supported, and individuals can thrive in the embrace of their own humanity.

Chapter 5

Effective Communication and Emotional Expression

Communication is the lifeblood of human connection, enabling us to express our thoughts, emotions, and needs with one another. Within the realm of mental health, effective communication and emotional expression play a pivotal role in fostering emotional well-being and maintaining meaningful relationships. In this chapter, we explore the importance of open and honest communication in the context of men's mental health. By understanding the barriers to communication, learning active listening skills, and embracing emotional vulnerability, men can forge deeper connections, navigate emotional challenges, and cultivate a healthier inner world.

The Importance of Communication in Mental Health:

Communication is a cornerstone of mental health, allowing individuals to share their feelings, seek support, and express their emotional needs. For men, societal norms around traditional masculinity may discourage open emotional expression, leading to communication challenges and feelings of isolation. Recognizing the significance of communication in mental wellness is essential for creating an environment where men feel safe to share their emotions and seek help when needed.

Benefits of Effective Communication in Mental Health:

- Reduces feelings of isolation and loneliness
- Encourages emotional expression and catharsis
- Builds trust and strengthens relationships
- Enhances emotional intelligence and self-awareness
- Facilitates problem-solving and conflict resolution

Barriers to Effective Communication:

Several barriers may impede effective communication, particularly for men. Societal expectations around traditional masculinity may lead to emotional repression, making it difficult for men to articulate their feelings openly. Fear of judgment or rejection may deter men from seeking emotional support, leading to a sense of emotional isolation. Misunderstandings arising from poor communication can also strain relationships and contribute to emotional distress.

Common Barriers to Effective Communication:

- Emotional repression due to traditional masculinity norms
- Fear of vulnerability and being perceived as weak
- Miscommunication and misunderstanding of emotions
- Social pressures to appear emotionally strong and invulnerable
- Lack of awareness or language to express complex emotions

Active Listening and Empathy:

Listening is an essential component of effective communication. Active listening involves fully engaging with the speaker, paying attention to both their words and non-verbal cues. By practising active listening, individuals demonstrate empathy and create a safe space for emotional expression. Empathy, the ability to understand and share the feelings of another, is a powerful tool for fostering emotional connections and supporting mental well-being.

Practising Active Listening:

- Maintaining eye contact and using attentive body language
- Refraining from interrupting or offering immediate solutions
- Paraphrasing and summarizing the speaker's thoughts and feelings
- Validating the speaker's emotions and experiences
- Showing empathy and understanding without judgment

Emotional Expression and Vulnerability:

Emotional expression and vulnerability are essential for mental well-being, allowing individuals to process their emotions and seek support. For men, embracing vulnerability can be particularly challenging due to societal expectations around traditional masculinity. However, the courage to express emotions openly and authentically is a sign of strength and self-awareness, paving the way for emotional growth and connection.

Embracing Emotional Expression:

- Recognizing and acknowledging emotions without judgment
- Finding safe spaces to express emotions, such as with trusted friends or in therapy

- Engaging in creative outlets to channel emotions constructively
- Developing emotional intelligence through self-reflection and self-awareness

Setting Boundaries and Self-Care in Communication:

Effective communication also involves setting boundaries and practising self-care. Men must recognize their emotional limits and communicate them to others to prevent burnout or emotional overwhelm. Understanding the importance of self-care in maintaining mental well-being is essential for fostering healthy communication habits.

Practising Self-Care and Setting Boundaries:

- Identifying emotional triggers and learning healthy coping mechanisms
- Communicating personal boundaries in relationships and interactions
- Taking time for self-care activities that promote emotional well-being
- Prioritizing mental health and seeking help when needed

Seeking Professional Support:

Despite the efforts to communicate effectively and express emotions, some challenges may require professional support. Mental health professionals can provide guidance, tools, and strategies for navigating through emotional difficulties and fostering healthier communication patterns.

When to Seek Professional Support:

- When communication challenges lead to relationship conflicts
- When emotional expression feels overwhelming or unmanageable
- When navigating significant life changes or losses
- When coping mechanisms become maladaptive or harmful

Effective communication and emotional expression are at the heart of mental wellness, promoting emotional resilience, and fostering meaningful connections. For men, breaking free from the confines of traditional masculinity norms is a powerful step toward embracing emotional vulnerability and authentic self-expression. By practising active listening, empathy, and openness, men can cultivate a compassionate inner dialogue and create a supportive environment for emotional well-being.

In a world where open communication is valued, men can find strength in embracing their emotions and seeking help when needed. Through self-awareness, self-care, and the courage to express emotions authentically, men can navigate the complexities of their inner world with grace and resilience. As we cultivate a society that encourages emotional expression and vulnerability, we pave the way for a brighter future where men can thrive in the embrace of their full emotional selves.

Chapter 6
Overcoming Barriers to Seeking Help

Seeking help for mental health challenges is an essential step towards emotional well-being and resilience. However, for many individuals, including men, various barriers can deter them from seeking the support they need. In this chapter, we explore the common barriers that may prevent men from reaching out for help, including societal expectations, stigma, and fear of judgment. By understanding and addressing these barriers, we aim to empower men to overcome obstacles and embrace the path towards healing and mental wellness.

Societal Expectations and Traditional Masculinity:

Societal expectations surrounding traditional masculinity can be a significant barrier to seeking help for mental health challenges. Men may feel pressure to conform to the image of stoicism and emotional restraint, fearing that seeking help will be perceived as a sign of weakness. The belief that men should "tough it out" or "handle it on their own" can prevent them from expressing vulnerability and seeking support.

Breaking Free from Traditional Masculinity Norms:

- Recognizing that vulnerability is a strength, not a weakness
- Challenging societal expectations and embracing emotional expression
- Surrounding oneself with supportive individuals who encourage seeking help

Stigma and Misconceptions about Mental Health:

Stigma surrounding mental health remains a pervasive issue that can prevent individuals from seeking help. The fear of being judged or labelled negatively may lead men to suffer in silence, avoiding discussions about their mental well-being. Additionally, misconceptions about mental health conditions can perpetuate stigma and create further barriers to seeking support.

Promoting Mental Health Awareness and Education:

- Engaging in mental health awareness campaigns to combat stigma
- Sharing personal stories of recovery and seeking help to reduce misconceptions
- Educating communities and workplaces about mental health to foster understanding

Fear of Judgement and Rejection:

The fear of judgment from others can prevent men from opening up about their mental health struggles. They may worry about how friends, family, or colleagues will perceive them if they seek help. The fear of rejection or isolation can be paralysing, leading men to internalize their emotions and avoid seeking support.

Creating Safe Spaces for Vulnerability:

- Building supportive networks of friends and loved ones who prioritize mental health
- Initiating open and non-judgmental conversations about mental health
- Seeking professional support from mental health providers who provide a safe and confidential environment

Self-Stigma and Internalized Shame:

Internalized shame and self-stigma can be significant barriers to seeking help. Men may struggle with feelings of inadequacy or failure, believing that they should be able to "handle" their problems independently. Self-stigma can lead to a reluctance to accept one's mental health challenges and a resistance to seeking help.

Practising Self-Compassion and Acceptance:

- Cultivating self-compassion and recognizing that seeking help is a courageous step

- Challenging self-stigmatizing thoughts and beliefs through cognitive-behavioural techniques
- Embracing imperfections and understanding that mental health challenges are part of being human

Lack of Knowledge about Available Resources:

The lack of knowledge about available mental health resources can be a significant obstacle to seeking help. Men may not be aware of the support services, counselling options, or helplines that exist to assist them in times of need.

Increasing Access to Mental Health Information:

- Providing accessible and comprehensive information about mental health resources
- Collaborating with community organizations to promote mental health services
- Utilizing digital platforms and social media to disseminate mental health information

Financial and Practical Concerns:

Financial constraints and practical concerns can deter men from seeking professional support for mental health challenges. The cost of therapy or counselling may be prohibitive, and men may face practical barriers such as scheduling conflicts or lack of transportation.

Addressing Financial and Practical Barriers:

- Exploring free or low-cost mental health services available in the community
- Seeking support from mental health organizations that provide financial assistance
- Advocating for workplace policies that prioritize employee

mental health

Overcoming barriers to seeking help is a crucial step in promoting mental wellness and fostering emotional resilience. By understanding and addressing the societal expectations, stigma, and fears that deter men from seeking support, we create an environment where emotional expression and vulnerability are embraced. Breaking free from the confines of traditional masculinity norms, men can prioritize their mental health and well-being, seeking help when needed without fear of judgment or rejection. Through mental health awareness, education, and compassionate dialogue, we empower men to recognize that seeking help is a courageous and strength-building step. By nurturing an environment that values emotional well-being and supports open communication, we pave the way for a future where men can navigate their emotional landscape with grace and resilience. As we address barriers and embrace mental health with understanding and compassion, we foster a society where seeking help is seen as a sign of self-awareness and strength.

Together, we create a culture of empathy, where individuals are encouraged to embrace their emotions, reach out for support, and embark on a journey towards healing and mental wellness.

Chapter 7
Supporting Men in Crisis

Crisis moments are an inevitable part of the human experience, and they can impact individuals of all genders, including men. During times of crisis, such as experiencing a loss, trauma, or overwhelming emotional distress, support and understanding play a vital role in facilitating recovery and emotional healing. In this chapter, we explore strategies for supporting men in crisis, acknowledging the unique challenges they may face due to societal expectations and traditional masculinity norms. By fostering a compassionate and empathetic approach, we can create an environment where men feel safe to express their emotions, seek help, and navigate through difficult times with resilience.

Recognizing Signs of Crisis:

The first step in supporting men in crisis is recognizing the signs of distress and emotional struggle. Men may be more likely to internalize their emotions and attempt to cope independently, making it crucial to pay attention to subtle cues and changes in behaviour.

Signs of Crisis in Men:

- Sudden changes in mood or behaviour
- Withdrawal from social activities and relationships
- Increased irritability or anger
- Changes in sleep patterns, such as insomnia or oversleeping
- Expressing feelings of hopelessness or worthlessness
- Engaging in risky behaviours, such as substance abuse or self-harm

Creating a Safe and Non-Judgmental Environment:

Supporting men in crisis requires creating a safe and non-judgmental environment where they feel comfortable expressing their emotions and seeking help. Breaking free from traditional masculinity norms involves challenging any beliefs or attitudes that stigmatize emotional vulnerability.

Fostering a Safe Environment:

- Encouraging open and honest communication about emotions and struggles
- Practising active listening and empathy without judgment
- Offering reassurance and validation for their emotions and experiences
- Being available for support and checking in on their well-being

Encouraging Professional Help:

In times of crisis, professional help from mental health providers can be invaluable in offering guidance and support. Men may be hesitant to seek professional help due to stigma or perceived weakness, but encouraging and normalizing therapy or counselling can be empowering.

Supporting Men in Seeking Professional Help:

- Educating them about the benefits of therapy or counselling
- Sharing stories of others who have benefited from professional support
- Offering to accompany them to their first therapy session for reassurance

Connecting with Support Networks:

During a crisis, social support is crucial for emotional well-being. Men may benefit from connecting with friends, family, or support groups who can provide understanding, empathy, and companionship.

Supporting Social Connections:

- Encouraging them to reach out to friends and loved ones for support
- Assisting in finding local support groups or mental health communities

- Arranging social activities or outings to foster connection

Practising Self-Care and Coping Strategies:
During a crisis, men can benefit from practising self-care and coping strategies to manage emotional distress. Encouraging healthy coping mechanisms can empower them to navigate through difficult emotions and challenges.

Promoting Self-Care:

- Suggesting relaxation techniques, such as mindfulness or deep breathing exercises
- Encouraging physical activity, which can boost mood and reduce stress
- Engaging in creative outlets, such as writing or art, as a form of expression and release

Respecting Boundaries and Autonomy:
In supporting men in crisis, it is essential to respect their boundaries and autonomy. While offering support, it is crucial not to pressure them into sharing more than they are comfortable with or imposing solutions on their situation.

Respecting Boundaries and Autonomy:

- Being mindful of their comfort level in discussing emotions and experiences
- Offering support and resources without pressuring them to disclose more than they are ready to share
- Trusting their judgment in making decisions about their well-being

Identifying and Addressing Safety Concerns:

In some crisis situations, safety concerns may arise, especially if there are thoughts of self-harm or harm to others. It is essential to take any safety concerns seriously and seek immediate professional help or involve appropriate authorities.

Addressing Safety Concerns:

- Asking directly about thoughts of self-harm or harm to others
- Encouraging them to contact a crisis helpline or mental health professional
- Involving emergency services or loved ones if necessary

Supporting men in crisis requires an approach that is empathetic, compassionate, and understanding of the challenges they may face due to societal expectations and traditional masculinity norms. By recognizing signs of distress, fostering a safe and non-judgmental environment, encouraging professional help, and promoting social connections and coping strategies, we can create a supportive network that empowers men to navigate through difficult times with resilience. As we break free from the confines of traditional masculinity norms and challenge stigma around mental health, we foster an environment where men can prioritize their emotional well-being and seek support without fear of judgment or weakness. Together, we build a society that embraces emotional expression, values mental wellness, and supports men in crisis with the compassion and understanding they deserve.

Chapter 8
Workplace Mental Health

The workplace is a significant aspect of our lives, where we spend a substantial amount of time and energy. As such, it has a profound impact on our mental well-being. Recognizing and prioritizing workplace mental health is crucial for creating a supportive and nurturing environment for employees. In this chapter, we explore the importance of workplace mental health, the impact of work-related stress on employees, and strategies to promote emotional well-being and resilience in the workplace.

Understanding the Importance of Workplace Mental Health:

Workplace mental health refers to the emotional well-being of employees in the context of their work environment. A positive workplace culture that values mental health can lead to increased job satisfaction, productivity, and overall well-being. Conversely, neglecting mental health in the workplace can lead to decreased performance, increased absenteeism, and higher turnover rates.

Benefits of Prioritizing Workplace Mental Health:

- Improved job satisfaction and employee morale
- Enhanced productivity and performance
- Reduced absenteeism and turnover rates
- Enhanced teamwork and collaboration
- Increased employee loyalty and retention

Identifying Work-Related Stress:

Work-related stress is a prevalent issue that can significantly impact employee mental health. High workload, tight deadlines, lack of autonomy, and workplace conflicts are some of the factors that contribute to work-related stress. Identifying and addressing sources of stress in the workplace is essential for promoting employee well-being.

Common Sources of Work-Related Stress:

- Excessive workload and unrealistic expectations

- Lack of work-life balance
- Inadequate support from managers or colleagues
- Unclear job expectations and role ambiguity
- Job insecurity and fear of lay-offs
- Bullying or harassment in the workplace
- Creating a Supportive Work Environment:

Fostering a supportive work environment is critical for promoting workplace mental health. Employers and managers play a crucial role in creating a culture that values mental well-being and encourages open communication.

Strategies to Create a Supportive Work Environment:

- Implementing flexible work arrangements to promote work-life balance
- Providing access to employee assistance programs and mental health resources
- Encouraging open communication about mental health and emotions
- Recognizing and celebrating employees' achievements and contributions
- Promoting a culture of empathy and understanding

Training and Education on Mental Health:
Educating employees and managers about mental health is an essential aspect of promoting workplace mental health. Mental health training can help employees recognize signs of distress in themselves and their colleagues, fostering a culture of support and compassion.

Benefits of Mental Health Training:

- Increased awareness and understanding of mental health challenges

- Improved ability to recognize signs of distress and offer support
- Reduced stigma surrounding mental health in the workplace
- Enhanced communication and emotional intelligence

Stress Management and Coping Strategies:

Providing employees with stress management and coping strategies can empower them to navigate work-related stress more effectively. These strategies can help employees build resilience and maintain emotional well-being during challenging times.

Stress Management Techniques for Employees:

- Mindfulness and meditation practices
- Time management and prioritization of tasks
- Physical exercise and relaxation techniques
- Seeking social support from colleagues or friends

- Engaging in hobbies or activities outside of work for stress relief

Promoting Work-Life Balance:

Maintaining a healthy work-life balance is essential for employee well-being. Employers can support work-life balance by offering flexible work schedules, remote work options, and ensuring employees can take breaks during the workday.

Benefits of Promoting Work-Life Balance:

- Reduced work-related stress and burnout
- Increased job satisfaction and morale
- Improved employee retention and loyalty
- Enhanced productivity and creativity

Addressing Workplace Bullying and Harassment:

Workplace bullying and harassment can have severe consequences on an employee's mental health. Employers must have clear policies in place to address such issues promptly and support affected employees.

Steps to Address Workplace Bullying and Harassment:

- Implementing anti-bullying and harassment policies
- Encouraging employees to report incidents without fear of retaliation
- Conducting thorough investigations and taking appropriate disciplinary actions
- Providing support and resources for affected employees

Offering Mental Health Benefits:

Providing mental health benefits as part of the employee benefits package demonstrates a commitment to prioritizing workplace mental health. Access to counselling services, therapy, and mental health resources can make a significant difference in employee well-being.

Benefits of Offering Mental Health Benefits:

- Improved access to mental health support for employees

- Enhanced employee satisfaction and loyalty
- Reduced stigma surrounding mental health
- Increased productivity and performance

Workplace mental health is a vital aspect of employee well-being and productivity. By understanding the impact of work-related stress, creating a supportive work environment, and offering stress management strategies and mental health benefits, employers can promote a culture that values mental wellness. Training and education on mental health can foster a culture of empathy and understanding, reducing stigma and encouraging open communication. By prioritizing workplace mental health, organizations not only improve employee satisfaction and retention but also cultivate a more productive and resilient workforce. Together, let us create a workplace environment where mental health is valued, and employees are supported in their journey towards emotional well-being and fulfilment.

Chapter 9
Navigating Life Transitions

MENTAL
HEALTH

Life is a series of transitions, marked by significant changes and milestones that shape our personal and professional paths. Whether it's graduating from school, starting a new job, getting married, becoming a parent, or retiring, life transitions can bring a mix of excitement, uncertainty, and emotional challenges. In this chapter, we explore the impact of life transitions on mental health, strategies for coping with change, and the importance of self-care and support during these transformative periods.

Understanding the Impact of Life Transitions:

Life transitions can evoke a range of emotions, from joy and anticipation to anxiety and fear. Each transition signifies a shift from one phase of life to another, involving adjustments to new roles, responsibilities, and environments. The stress of adapting to change, along with the uncertainty of the future, can impact mental health and well-being.

Common Life Transitions:

- Graduating from school or college
- Starting a new job or career change
- Getting married or entering into a committed relationship
- Becoming a parent or experiencing empty nest syndrome
- Relocating to a new city or country
- Retiring from work

Coping with Change and Uncertainty:

Coping with life transitions involves embracing change and managing the accompanying uncertainty. Resilience and adaptability are key traits that can help individuals navigate through these periods of transformation.

Strategies for Coping with Change:

- Practising mindfulness to stay grounded in the present

moment

- Setting realistic expectations for oneself during the transition
- Seeking support from friends, family, or a therapist
- Engaging in self-reflective practices to better understand emotions and needs
- Maintaining a sense of humour to find lightness in the midst of change

Building Resilience and Emotional Strength:

Resilience is the ability to bounce back from challenges and adapt positively to life's changes. Building resilience is essential for navigating life transitions with emotional strength and perseverance.

Building Resilience:

- Cultivating a growth mindset, focusing on learning and personal growth
- Engaging in activities that promote emotional well-being, such as exercise and hobbies
- Finding meaning and purpose in the transition and the new phase of life
- Seeking support from others to build a strong support network
- Practising self-compassion and embracing imperfections

Managing Stress and Anxiety:

Life transitions can be accompanied by heightened stress and anxiety, especially when facing unknowns or significant life changes. Managing stress and anxiety during these periods is crucial for maintaining mental well-being.

Stress Management Techniques:

- Deep breathing exercises and relaxation techniques
- Time management and prioritizing tasks

- Engaging in physical activity to release tension
- Expressing emotions through journaling or creative outlets
- Seeking professional help for persistent anxiety or overwhelming stress

Embracing Self-Care during Transitions:

During life transitions, self-care becomes even more crucial in nurturing mental and emotional well-being. Taking intentional steps to care for oneself can provide a sense of stability and comfort during times of change.

Self-Care Practices:

- Getting enough rest and prioritizing sleep
- Eating nutritious foods to support physical and emotional health
- Engaging in activities that bring joy and relaxation

- Practising mindfulness and meditation for emotional grounding
- Setting boundaries and taking breaks when needed

Seeking Support from Others:

Seeking support from others is an essential aspect of navigating life transitions. Friends, family, and support groups can offer understanding, encouragement, and perspective during times of change.

Support Systems:

- Sharing feelings and experiences with trusted friends or family members
- Joining support groups related to the specific life transition
- Seeking guidance from mentors or role models who have experienced similar transitions

- Considering individual or group therapy for additional support

Embracing Change as an Opportunity for Growth:
Life transitions offer an opportunity for growth, self-discovery, and new beginnings. Embracing change as a chance to explore new possibilities and expand one's horizons can foster a positive mindset during these transformative periods.

Embracing Change as an Opportunity:

- Emphasizing the positive aspects of the transition and its potential benefits
- Setting new goals and aspirations for the future
- Recognizing that change is a natural part of life's journey
- Embracing curiosity and a sense of adventure in the face of uncertainty

Life transitions are an integral part of the human experience, shaping our personal and professional paths. Understanding the impact of life transitions on mental health and implementing coping strategies can help individuals navigate through periods of change with resilience and emotional strength. By embracing self-care, seeking support from others, and viewing change as an opportunity for growth, individuals can navigate life transitions with grace and a sense of empowerment.

Together, let us recognize the transformative power of life transitions and embrace these moments as stepping stones toward greater self-awareness, fulfilment, and emotional well-being.

Conclusion

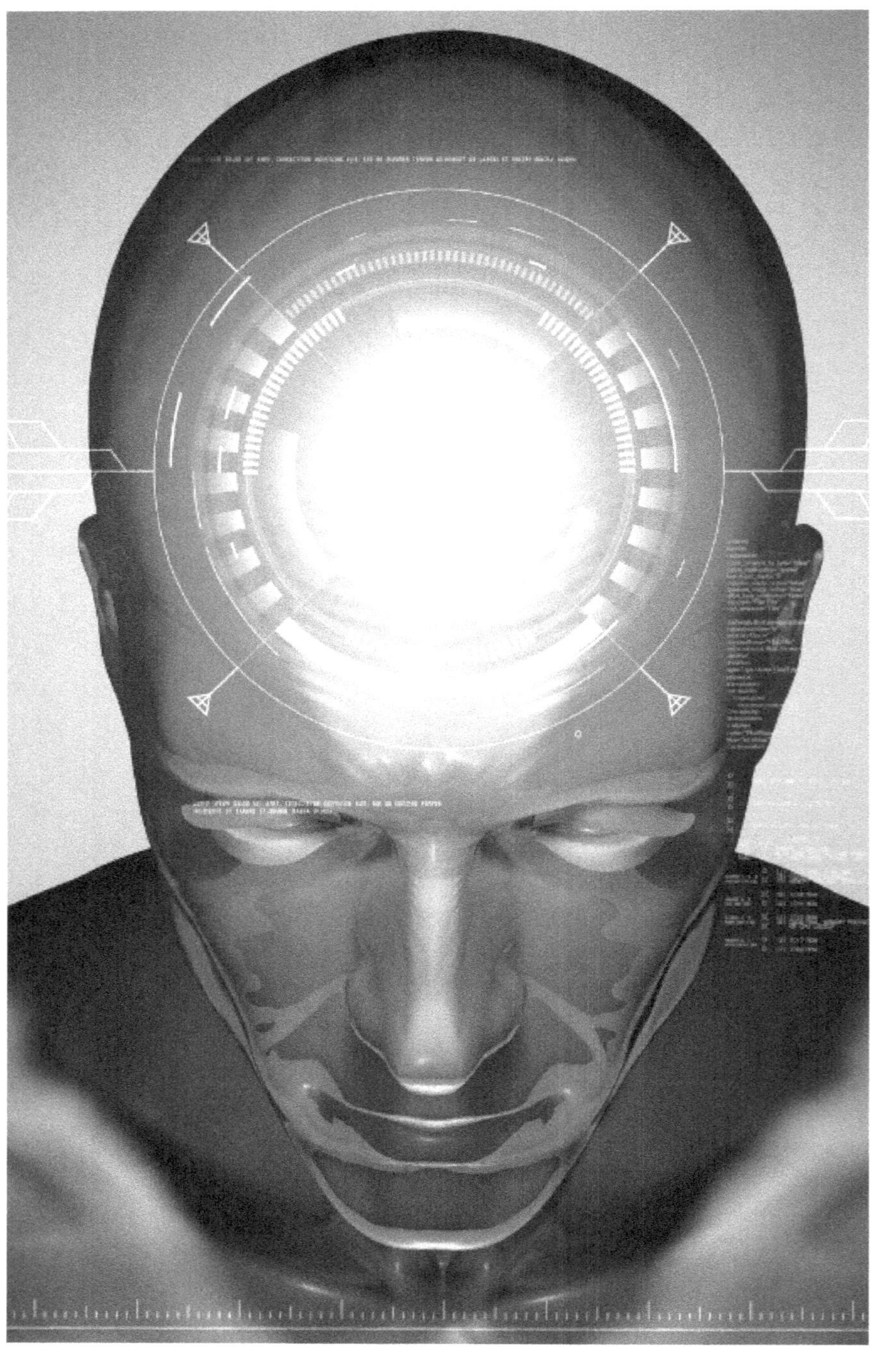

In "Mental Health Awareness: A Comprehensive Guide to Mental Health for Men," we embarked on a journey to explore the complexities of men's mental well-being, dismantle the barriers to seeking help, and promote emotional resilience and connection. Throughout this book, we delved into the significance of understanding mental health, the impact of gender norms on men's emotional well-being, common mental health challenges, promoting mental wellness, supporting men in crisis, and navigating life transitions. Our exploration was grounded in the belief that fostering mental health awareness and support is not only a collective responsibility but also a pathway to personal growth and fulfilment.

As we conclude this guide, I want to emphasize that mental health is a vital aspect of every individual's overall well-being, regardless of gender. Men, too, deserve to be supported, heard, and understood in their emotional journey. Let us break free from the confines of traditional masculinity norms and embrace emotional expression as a sign of strength, self-awareness, and courage. I encourage you, dear readers, to take the knowledge and insights gained from this book and put them into action. Let us strive to create an environment where mental health is valued, where vulnerability is embraced, and where seeking help is seen as an act of self-care and empowerment.

If this book has resonated with you and provided valuable insights, I kindly request that you take a moment to share your thoughts in a review. Your feedback can help others discover this guide and find support in their own mental health journey.

Together, let us build a society that prioritizes mental well-being, fosters understanding and compassion, and supports every individual, regardless of gender, in their pursuit of emotional health and resilience. May this book serve as a stepping stone towards a world where mental health awareness is embraced, and men can navigate life's challenges with grace, authenticity, and the knowledge that they are not alone.

Thank you for joining me on this journey. Let us continue to shine a light on mental health matters and create a world where emotional well-being is valued and nurtured.

With gratitude and hope,

Dr. Jilesh